I Was PROMiSED a BAby

a storybook guide for new dads

^hilarious

^and soon to be

By **Carlos Puga**

Illustrations by **Javier Gimenez Ratti**

I Was Promised a Baby

STANDARD ARTS

First Edition

ALL RIGHTS RESERVED

PRINTED IN THE PRC

ISBN: 978-0-578-46482-4

Illustrations by Javier Gimenez Ratti

Neither the author nor the publisher is engaged in rendering professional advice or services to individual readers. The ideas and suggestions contained in this book are not intended as substitute for consulting with a professional, be it medical or otherwise. Neither the author nor the publisher shall be liable or responsible for any loss or damage allegedly arising from any information contained in this book. But, come on, shouldn't that go without saying? I mean, the author can barely tie his shoes, he flosses maybe twice a year, is he someone you would seriously heed life advice from? Grow up.

Furthermore, the author is in no way endorsing any attempts of herculean physical undertakings by amateurs, and accepts no liability for injuries (or even death) resulting from the running of marathons by non-marathoners or from motorcycle accidents in the Andes mountains by the untrained. Yes, you read that right. The author would like to take this moment to also proclaim that we need not be confined by the paradigms we endure day-in and day-out. Paradigms like "the tiny copy on the first page of a book is limited to legal jargon and copyright information". No, that is just something you've held true solely because of your past experience with such pages. But I am here to tell you the truth: there are no rules. It's all bullshit.

The author would now like to acknowledge that although it is not a widely adopted practice, brushing one's teeth in the shower makes a lot of sense. He would also like to disclose (strictly as an example, and not as a way of "showing off" —because the author is not that type of person—) that in 2017 he ran a marathon; a bona fide marathon in a major American city known for its lovely weather. And that he decided to run that marathon three days before said event. And that prior to running this marathon, the farthest he had ever run in one stretch was maybe 2 miles, once. The author would also like to tell you, the reader, that he detests running more than invasive dental work, and that he has never "jogged" or done any sort of fitness routine other than random recreational sports here and there. And yet he did, in fact, run this marathon. On three-days' notice. And that he only ran the damn thing because he woke up one day, saw a billboard for it and felt like giving it a shot. A "bucket list" kind of thing. "If not now, when?" sort of thing. And the author admits that when he saw the billboard and the idea first struck him, it was a mere thought, a "perhaps" sort of thing, but that the thought quickly became a steadfast decision when he heard people's reactions to it: "Pff, you can't run a marathon, get real!", "Yeah right, you have to train for *months* to run a marathon!". The scoffs were endless. Even my own notions of who could or could not do what held me back.

I mean, no way a guy like me could just decide to run a *marathon* one day, right?

The author would like to connect the dots here and tell you that this seemingly trite accomplishment of his should prove to you not only that: A) Roadside advertising works, but (more importantly) B) The notions you have in your head about things out-of-reach or out of the realm of possibility are bullshit. People in positions of power thrive by creating an air of exclusionary expertise around what they do, things unattainable for the common man, but it is all bullshit. Granted, it took me a shade over 5 hours to finish the marathon, and it hurt like hell toward the end, but I did it. And the feeling I got when I crossed the finish line was one I'll never forget. The author is not ashamed to admit it, he got emotional, maybe even shed a tear. And the feeling he felt during those three days leading up to the event, the nervousness inherent before a truly NEW endeavor, before a major test; it is a feeling he often felt as a young person, but a feeling that sadly has shown itself more and more seldom later in life; which is why he thinks we should strive for it every now and again, regardless of age. At the risk of now actually "showing off" or trying to sound "cool", the author would also like to tell you that he has every now and again taken up other personal challenges in that same vein: to solidify a notion that has grown in the author's head—that our very definition of ourselves can/should evolve from time to time. The feats range from the mundane (trying olives for the first time, and actually loving them!) to the stupid and irresponsible (crossing Patagonia on a motorcycle by himself). And then *this*. This book. Yes, that same notion is why the author wrote this book. Because when the idea began, people scoffed and said "You can't just *write* a book." and then made a funny contortion of their eyebrows. But really, actually, yes I can. Anyone can. I too used to mystify a great many things. I too would think running marathons required something *special*; and the writing of books was for those who had been *chosen* at birth in some secret, sacred ceremony. But look at this, my own book, in your hands. And you're reading it!

Lastly, the author would like to admit that he totally stole this whole "writing prose in tiny font in the "legal" or "copyright" section of the book" from one of his favorite books. And that he not only stole the *idea* itself, but also kinda copied the *style* as best he could because he likes it so much; including the rampant use of italics and quotation marks to emphasize certain words with a little '*flair*'. He won't mention the book by name, having no idea whether that book's author would appreciate or frown upon such meddling; but if you're really curious about the name of said book, send me an email and I'll tell you. My email address shouldn't be hard to either find or surmise, knowing that I published this book through my company (mentioned above).

In short, that which you think is impossible or limited to others, is not. Everything is everything.

For Meredith and Charlie

Before you arrived
life was simply divine.
Mom and I had it all,
we were perfectly fine.

We'd travel the globe
and paint the town red;
have fun all the time,
outdoors and in bed!

But everything changed
on one fateful day.
Mom yelled from the bathroom:
"Come here, right away!"

I ran down the hall
and what did I see?
A little blue X
all covered in pee.

"Impossible!" I said,
"Of this there's no doubt!
For even when drunk,
I always pull out!"

"This time you were late!"
Mom said; it was true,
I was promised a baby
after one careless screw.

Not long after that,
the first hiccup came:
mom woke up barfing
and cursing my name.

Then daddy's weenie
got locked in a vault;
shunned and forgotten
like all was his fault.

Life for your mommy
got tougher from there.
Carrying a baby
is hard work, I swear.

Her clothes didn't fit,
she ached in her spine,
her anger increased
each month without wine.

This torment went on
for half of a year.
Until at long last,
your due date was near.

Mom hated that last month,
she'd look down and shout:
"I was promised a baby,
hurry up and GET OUT!"

6

One night I awoke
from a weird little dream,
to a powerful shake
and a deafening scream.

"Go get the car!",
mom yelled in my ear.
"And hurry it up,
or I'll give birth right here!"

PRO TIP: Have a Go-Bag
prepared at week 36.
Learn more on page 35.

7

The docs offered drugs
to help with her pain.
Mom said for your sake
she'd politely refrain.

But with every contraction
mom grew more distraught.
Until she yelled "F*CK IT,
JUST GIVE ME THE SHOT!"

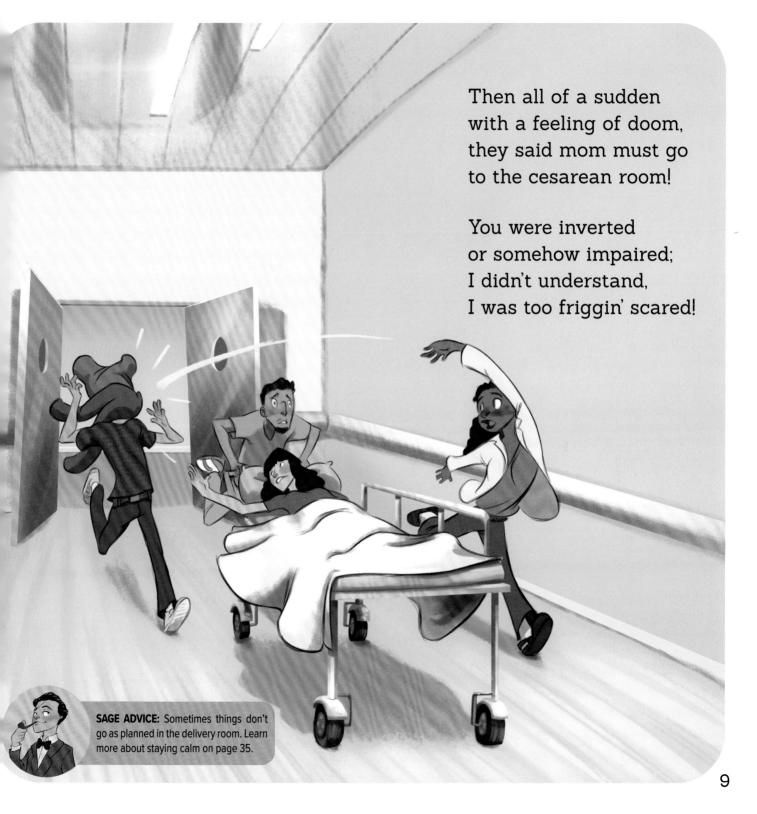

Then all of a sudden
with a feeling of doom,
they said mom must go
to the cesarean room!

You were inverted
or somehow impaired;
I didn't understand,
I was too friggin' scared!

SAGE ADVICE: Sometimes things don't go as planned in the delivery room. Learn more about staying calm on page 35.

9

The doctor inside
cut mommy just right;
and that's when your dad
went out like a light.

But daddy woke up
in time for your birth;
it's the gnarliest thing
I've seen on this Earth.

PRO TIP: If you're prone to fainting,
try concentrating on mom's face
during delivery. More on page 35.

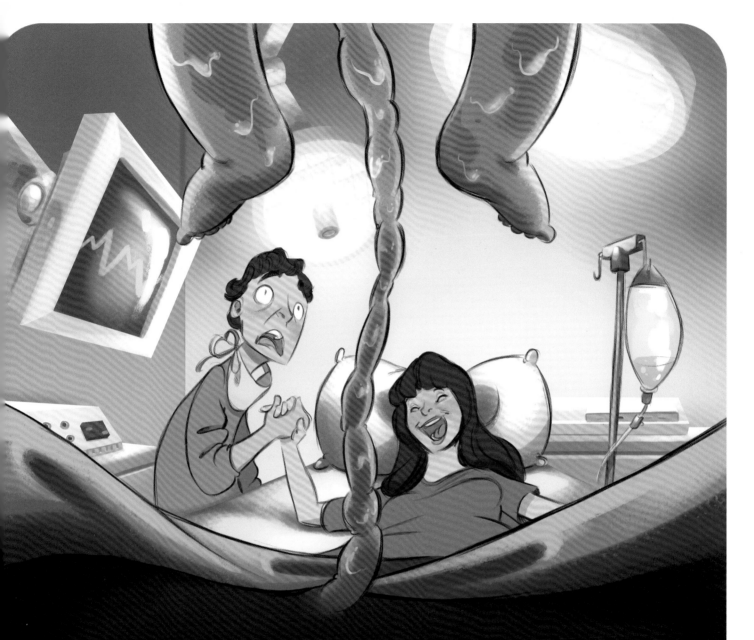

Of all the surprises,
here's the biggest, bar-none:
when a human is born
it looks only half-done.

I was promised a baby,
a cute little boo.
But you looked like a scrotum,
all wrinkled and blue.

The next couple days
I slept on a cot
while things like breastfeeding
and swaddling were taught.

The nurses got mad
and sneered when I said:
"This child is misshapen,
what's wrong with its head?!"

Then life changed a lot
for me and my hound.
I was promised a baby,
not ear-piercing sound.

The crying and wailing
endured day and night;
and every new sob
was cause for a fight.

13

There was tons of new work;
many diapers, unclean.
I swear I had never
seen poop that was green.

And the crap babies need,
we had no way of knowing.
The fortune we spent
kept growing and growing!

One weird contraption
that got me distressed
was a breast-pumping bra
strapped onto mom's chest.

Electrically charged
and wrapped up in tubes,
she looked like a robot
shooting milk from her boobs.

But I reached my wit's end
when I walked in and saw
mom slurping your boogers
through a clear curvy straw.*

I said "Now that's it!
I can't take any more!
I was promised a baby,
not poop, snot and gore!"

* This is a real thing.

16

That's how it continued:
more fights and no rest.
And you had sole access
to mom's swollen breast.

But latching and feeding
were not your forté;
you gave mom mastitis
four times just in May.

MAS·TI·TIS | \ ma-'stī-təs
inflammation of the mammary gland in the breast, typically due to bacterial infection, common when breastfeeding. More on page 40.

To tell you the truth,
things got pretty bleak.
I started to think
maybe I was a freak.

What I had expected
to some kind of degree
is that fatherly love
that I'd seen on TV.

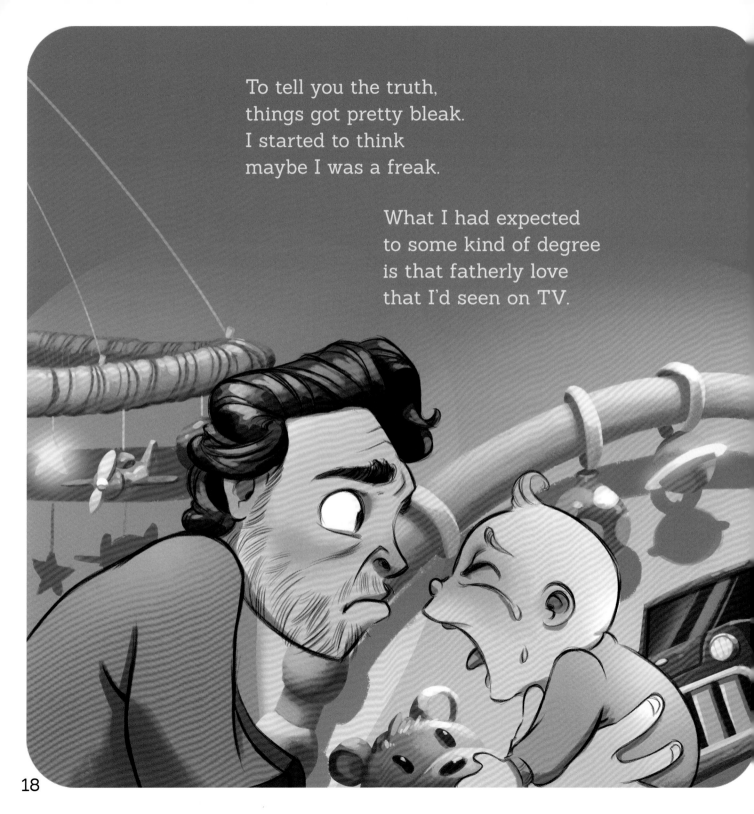

18

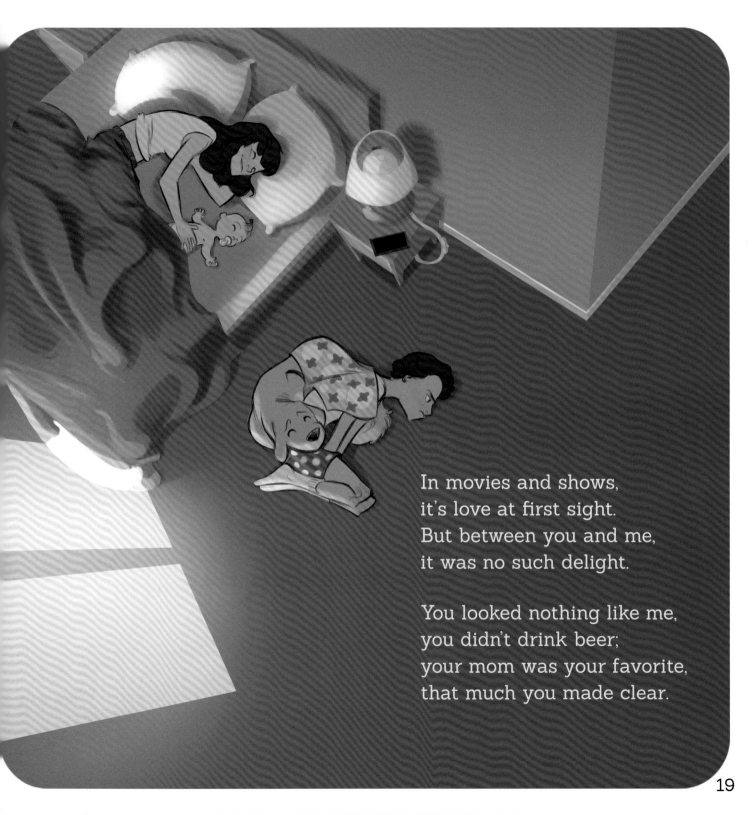

In movies and shows,
it's love at first sight.
But between you and me,
it was no such delight.

You looked nothing like me,
you didn't drink beer;
your mom was your favorite,
that much you made clear.

Then one Friday night,
you woke from your sleep.
And hungry as always,
you started to weep.

I fed you in silence
feeling FOMO galore,
the boys were all clowning
like I used to before.

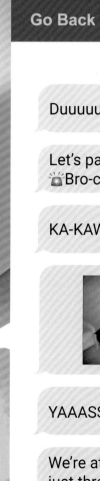

IWPAB 11:37 PM 55%

Go Back **BroThread** Photos

Today

Duuuuuuuuudes!!!!!

Let's party tonight!
🚨Bro-call🚨

KA-KAWWWW!!!!!

YAAASSS!!!!!!!

We're at Alex's. McCabe
just threw up lol

Text   Send

But as I read all the texts
and scrolled through my feed,
something far more important
did happen indeed ...

You paused from your bottle,
looked up for a while;
then, as if just for me,
you smiled your first smile.

I can't quite explain it;
that smile changed all.
My whole heart just melted
and I started to bawl.

A corner was turned;
our standoff had passed.
I was promised a baby
and I had one at last!

Our connection grew stronger
each day after that,
as you giggled and crawled
and you ate and you sat.

All the milestones
were accomplished, all right.
We shed tears of joy
when you slept through the night.

So yes, from then on
you ran the whole house.
And for months* I did not
touch my beautiful spouse.

Every time daddy tried
to get back his groove,
you'd interrupt
like you didn't approve.

* Times may vary.

But as the months passed,
we figured things out.
We balanced our schedule
and ended our drought!

By the time that you took
your first step and walked,
we were parenting pros;
our family rocked!

So to all of you dads
who need some support,
here's one little thing
I've learned in this sport:

Despite feeling strained
for the first ninety days,
help out with the chores and
show mom some praise ...*

* She's the one doing
most of the work, dude!

26

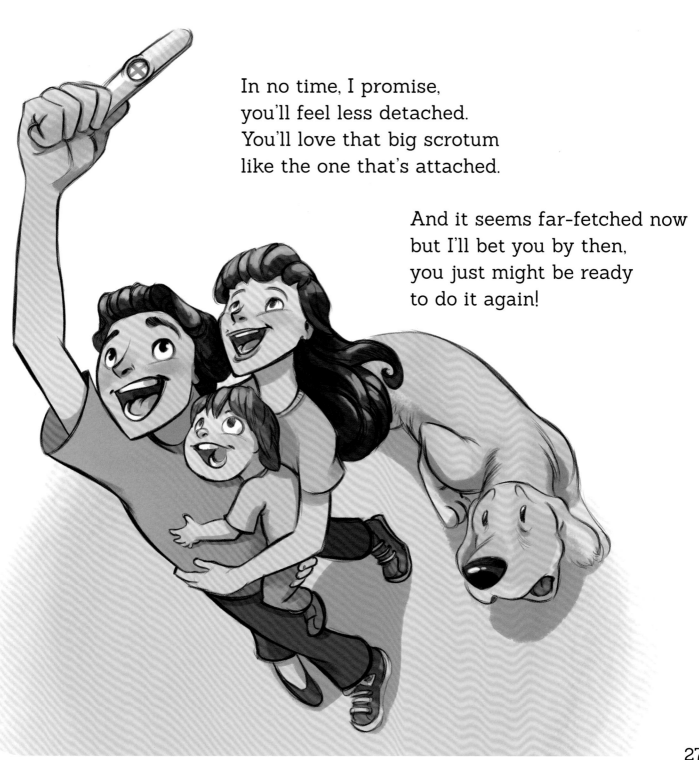

In no time, I promise,
you'll feel less detached.
You'll love that big scrotum
like the one that's attached.

And it seems far-fetched now
but I'll bet you by then,
you just might be ready
to do it again!

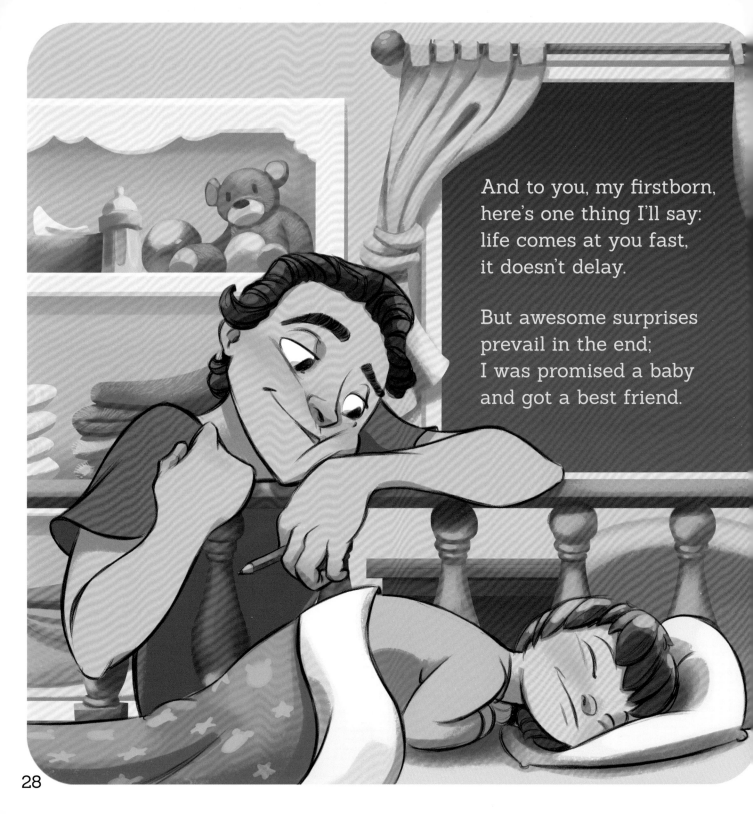

And to you, my firstborn,
here's one thing I'll say:
life comes at you fast,
it doesn't delay.

But awesome surprises
prevail in the end;
I was promised a baby
and got a best friend.

28

The End

APPENDIX

The (slightly) More Serious Part of the Book

Ok, so here's the thing, when my wife got pregnant, I was gifted several books aimed at expectant fathers. Each one had an unquestionably clever title (you've never seen more puns conflating the words Dude and Dad in your life) and was hefty enough to give it the appropriate gravitas for the occasion (no less than 200 pages). But all that cleverness and density notwithstanding, the sad truth is, I didn't actually read any of those books. Never made it past the foreword. Didn't even open some.

I'm not saying these books were not worthwhile; reading a comprehensive book before embarking on a monumental life experience is not a bad idea at all (it's probably pretty responsible and thoughtful actually), but it's just not my bag. For example, let's say I was about to move from NYC to Seattle; useful as it may be, I wouldn't read a big book on moving across the country. Some people might feel the

need, just not me. I'd prefer to do some personal research beforehand, then figure things out along the way.

Which is why I wrote this book. *For us!* Because while I was not inclined to read a laborious, cover-to-cover how-to about having a baby, I certainly was curious and enthused, and I definitely would have read something that was a little more quickly digestible. Especially if it included some laughs. Something to give me some basics. A cheat-sheet of sorts. Something fun and easy. Lay a little groundwork. Leave me to do some further digging on my own.

I guess what I'm trying to say is that this book was written for the *right* reasons. I want you to know I am in this with *you*. I want you to know that the eventual fame, fortune and (albeit long-overdue) recognition as a "once-in-a-generation literary juggernaut" that will undoubtedly envelop me once this book is out in the world—all that is simply a byproduct, a side-effect of the enterprise, never its primary objective. After all, how could I have known? How could anyone have known?

No, I did this for you. And no matter how rich or famous I get, or how impossible I will forevermore be to *reach*, please know that we will always be *in this together*.

And another thing: I'd like to put it out there that my wife deserves most of the credit for our first year of child rearing. No matter how many books I had read, no written word can truly prepare you for having a baby. And as the illustrations in this book demonstrate, I was a bumbling fool much of the time, taking her courageous lead and learning from her. My hope is that this book might help you do a little better. That said though, I'd also like to make clear that there were some artistic liberties taken in the form of exaggeration when it comes to dad's distress and bungling in this book, all in the name of humor. Don't worry guys, it's not that bad. You'll do fine.

Now, lest I turn our fun little project here into actual "work" by trying to saturate it with "useful information", let me just say this:

In this day and age, a quick web search on any of the topics discussed herein will undoubtedly generate a more than ample supply of informative reading materials; each surely more thorough, professional, verifiable and perhaps plain *better* than those offered in this book. Some maybe even written by scholars, doctors, or perhaps authors with more *experience* or *expertise* than your humble narrator (yet none with more flair or joie de vivre, let's face it); but still.

There's a lot of reference books for new parents out there. If you are looking for A-to-Z instructions, believe me, you won't have to look far. Sadly though, I won't be able to cite or recommend any specific books here because a) Like I said, I didn't read any, and b) I'm still pretty hazy on the legality of citing private persons, companies, or other entities by name in this book. Do I, say, need Apple's consent to print the fact that I dig their laptops? And now that I've gone ahead and done so, will they be flattered and thus feel compelled to send me free ones (please)? Or perhaps they won't dig it at all and instead they'll sue?! Ruin us financially? I guess we'll find out! You and me! Because we're in this *together*, remember!

Point is, when it comes to research, nowadays you can curate your own experience. So let this book be one source for you. Have a laugh, get a feel for some of my experience, then go on and read all the other material your little heart desires.

Oh, and before I forget: I am no expert in any of this crap. Any actual health concerns or serious parenting questions should be answered by a professional, not a storybook parody. I mean, do I even have to say that?

So anyways, here's what I'm gonna do: the next few pages are going to be a bit of a recap of the storybook; except this time I'll include some useful info about the milestones that were illustrated therein. That way you can flip back and forth, between the notes and the corresponding illustration, holding a page with a finger maybe. Perhaps with a pen in your mouth. Or behind your ear. Like you're in a library, studying for the bar. Or a 19th century scholar, flipping to and fro, cross-referencing and whatnot. It'll be great.

Ok, here we go.

Page 3, THE POSITIVE PREGNANCY TEST: Finding out you're pregnant is an exciting, emotional, and maybe even scary moment for each (and both) of you. Contrary to this book's depiction of the event, I was happy upon hearing the news (we had been trying to get pregnant for a while actually). However, aside from feeling happiness, you might also feel nervous, or scared, or maybe even a little bummed on some level. Don't worry, it's a lot to try and process at once; and there's no right or wrong way to feel. If you are feeling less than psyched, maybe try and talk about it with someone, figure out exactly what you're feeling and why.

Page 4, MORNING SICKNESS: Once she gets pregnant, mom's body undergoes a lot of changes. During those first few weeks, there'll be hormone shifts, changes in blood sugar levels, bouts of stress, and a bunch of other pleasantries. Because of how these changes affect the body's normal chemistry, sometimes newly pregnant women have spells of nausea and/or vomiting. Despite it being called "Morning Sickness", the nausea and vomiting can occur at any time of the day or night (Yay!). It is something most women will experience at least once during pregnancy (though some lucky ones don't experience it at all). You can find exhaustive lists online of what to do or what to eat (or even smell) to help assuage the effects of morning sickness. Some say broths are a good remedy, as well as soft foods like rice. If it becomes a persistent problem, you guys should do some research and find a remedy that works for mom.

Page 5, PREGNANCY AND HORMONES: If wild mood swings occur, if she unnecessarily stokes an argument about some random, insignificant thing, if she cries at seemingly ridiculous things, always keep in mind that not only is there a raging river of hormones churning inside her, but she's also PREGNANT WITH A HUMAN. Cut her some slack. And pick your battles carefully. Or try not to pick them at all. Also, if/when she snaps at you in front of people, I would not recommend responding by saying things like "Oh she's just hormonal.", then blowing out your cheeks and making a balloon-belly gesture.

THE 3 STAGES: Pregnancy is divided into three trimesters. Each trimester is 3-months long, genius. In general, the first includes some discomfort for mom as her body adjusts to this new undertaking. The second trimester is called the 'honeymoon period'; it's when mom generally feels better (the nausea typically subsides), her emotions even out, her sex drive returns (yay!), and it is also when the baby's movements are first felt. Then comes the third trimester, when the baby is pretty big, it's ready to come out, hormones are churning, and mom starts to get uncomfortable again.

Page 6, THE LAST MONTH OF PREGNANCY: The last few weeks are no picnic for some moms; hormones start to kick back in and the body can start to get really uncomfortable (the baby is no longer the size of a peach). So try to pay extra attention to her comfort level and her needs; make an effort.

Page 7, GOING INTO LABOR: Unless you're having a scheduled C-section, you're not gonna know exactly when the baby is coming; accordingly, it's a good idea to pack a bag for the hospital beforehand (week 36 or 37) so it's ready and waiting when the moment arrives. On average, you'll be spending 2–3 nights in the hospital, so along with whatever you need for yourself (clothes, toiletries, etc), the bag should include things for mom like: Her Photo ID, insurance card, hospital forms; Couple pairs of (nonskid) socks; Hair tie; Non-perishable snacks; Flat shoes; Comfortable going-home clothes; Toiletries; A robe; Cell phone and charger. Also, it might be a good idea to leave the bag in the car so you don't forget it at home.

Pages 8 & 9, THE HOSPITAL: Hopefully everything goes swell and your little one pops out in no time; but (as in our case) sometimes shit happens. It's good to keep in mind that hospitals do this dozens of times a day and have highly trained professionals ready to deal with any unforeseen circumstance. If things don't go as planned, try to remain cool and roll with the punches; your composure will go a long way to helping mom remain calm. Remember: the only thing that matters here is the health of mom and the baby!

Page 10, THE DELIVERY: Knowing that I'm prone to fainting at the sight of blood, I immediately focused on my wife's face during the C-Section. It was a foolproof way to avoid seeing the gore and be a doting, caring husband to boot! There's still a lot of blood going around though, so stay focused. If you do feel a little queasy, be sure to tell a nurse and have a seat, last thing you wanna do is complicate matters by faceplanting into the birth. Once the baby is born, you'll probably be asked if you'd like to cut the umbilical cord. Despite my delicate constitution, I was able to do this without any issues. I found it more weird than anything, like cutting through a thick gummy worm.

Page 11, BABY'S FIRST BREATH: For obvious reasons, when you see a birth in a movie or TV show, you're probably not seeing a newborn, but instead an older (and cuter) baby in its place. Having never seen an <u>actual</u> newborn, a lot of dads don't know what to expect. So let me clue you in on a couple things: in order to fit through the birth canal, babies' heads have to be sort of squished (it's fine, they are designed to do this, the skull is not yet fused), so don't be surprised if your little one doesn't have a perfect little round head when he/she comes out. They are also probably going to be discolored, covered in lots of goo and blood, and not very happy at all. In short, they might look pretty unattractive (especially compared to the chubby little baby you might have pictured in your head). Don't worry though, they will get cleaned up, and they'll grow out of their tadpole phase very quickly. Heck, I bet you might even miss their little conehead when it's gone!

Page 12, THE HOSPITAL STAY: You'll probably be spending a couple nights in the hospital, sleeping on a cot from WWII (complete with exposed springs whose sharp points will be ready to jolt you back in to consciousness just as you're ready to doze off). Don't worry though, sleep won't happen for very long anyway, nurses will be coming in every few hours to have mom breastfeed the babe. During these couple days you'll also be getting a huge amount of information given to you by all sorts of doctors and nurses. Try to retain as much as you can, but don't worry, most of it will be repeated many times over the coming weeks/months. And if you have any questions, you can always call your doctor.

Page 13, THE HOMECOMING: Well, this is it. You've made it! Baby's out and the three of you are all at home. Congrats, the hard part is over!

LOL. This is when the work begins. The shift in your everyday life is going to be tremendous. For most people, the change in sleep schedule is by far the most shocking. The baby will need to be fed several times a night. Even if mom is the one forced to get up to breastfeed, you should still help her out. Be available. Or if she lets you sleep (like my saint of a wife did), make sure you are eager to help out in the morning when she is tired from a long night. Fights during this period are natural, you're both not sleeping, you have no idea what you're doing, and you're constantly worrying about whether or not baby is breathing. Those frazzled nerves are bound to cause some friction. Just try and take a couple minutes of alone time here and there to breathe, get things in perspective; you have a beautiful baby! And keep in mind that your partner is also going through some serious shit. Instead of turning on each other, try to unify as a team!

Page 14–16, THE GADGETS AND GIZMOS: No matter how low-maintenance you are, there are going to be some things you'll need to acquire when you have a baby. Don't worry, you won't have to buy all of them, many will probably come as gifts chosen from your registry (a long list of things you want friends and family to buy for you). Along with these registry gifts, there will also probably be a-la-carte things given to you by people who will swear their gift "saved their life" when they had a little one. Keep in mind though that all babies are different, as are all parents and parenting styles; some gadgets will be useful to some, and go unused by others. You won't know what works with your particular baby and style until you try them. And I recommend trying them all, because you never know what random thing might just make your baby happy.

Here's a few things my wife and I found most useful:

Bassinet: We used one of those high-tech, expensive smart bassinet-thingies, and we loved it. I don't know if I can say it by name, so I'll just tell you it rhymes with moo. The idea behind these things is this: babies wake up several times a night to feed, so waking up is inevitable; however, the process of getting your baby back to sleep can be taken out of your weary hands. This thing magically shakes and sways and plays some soothing sounds that put the babe right back to sleep almost as soon as you put him/her back in there, which saves you a nice chunk of time to be asleep. It also soothes the baby all night long with sounds and movement so the random wake-ups occur less often.

Carrying Devices: I'm not big on those front back-pack thingies where the baby dangles attached to your chest. But one was indispensable in order to stay active and do things like grocery shop, walk around the block, etc. My wife received one at first that you wrap or tie onto yourself, and she hated it; got rid of that fast. The front backpack one though she used every single day until Charlie was about 6 months old. We later (when Charlie's neck wasn't jelly and he could actually hold his head up) graduated to an old-school backpack thingy, which we use on hikes and walks. We found one from the 80s because they have less hardware than the newer ones.

Booger Sucker: I don't know if this was mandatory, but we did, in fact, purchase a little tube with which to suck the baby's snot out of his nose. The nostrils are too small to pick with a finger, and the boogers gotta come out, so you're gonna have to just man up and suck it out. Don't worry, the tube comes with a serious filter so none of the snot actually gets to your mouth.

Stroller: There's so many out there that you're probably gonna have to do your own research. We chose ours based on its simplicity and ability to transform into briefcase-mode at the touch of a button. And strangely enough, we don't even use it that much.

Car Seat: You have to have one. Nowadays all cars are made with latch systems inside the backseats so they're pretty easy to put in and take out. This is a purchase you probably want to do a little research on to find what's right for your car/lifestyle.

Jolly Jumper: I know I've made careful work so far of not naming any products by their brand names (so as to avoid lawsuits, etc.). So logic might dictate that I just call this thing "The Happy Hopper" or something; but I'm gonna say screw it and use the brand name when it comes to The Jolly Jumper, because it's the tits. It's a little seat for the baby that's connected to a chain and a spring. You can hang it from doorways or ceiling beams, etc, then put the little guy/girl in the seat, and watch them bungee up and down, suspended by the spring. For about 9 months, this thing was good for at least an hour of parental free time a day. And believe me, that is HUGE. That said, however, like all gizmos, not all babies will have the same reaction to it. Though our boy loved it, yours might hate it.

Baby Cam: Here's strange little factoid that you may or may not know depending on whether or not you are married—Ready? Renting a hundred chairs for a birthday party from a rental house will usually cost you about a third as much as renting the exact same hundred chairs from the exact same rental house for a wedding. It's true. There's a premium you pay for anything wedding related. Why? I guess it's because we're all saps and the rental guys know we'll shell anything out for our "special day" (especially if we're choosing those chairs in front of the bride-to-be and her mom). Well, I've found that the same is sometimes true for baby stuff. For example, when it came time to buy a camera/baby monitor, I looked at ones that cost anywhere from $79 to upwards of $350. Now, there may well be some features unbeknownst to me on some of those cameras that maybe justify their higher price, but I instead bought a $30 one that was touted as a "Pet Camera",

38

and it's worked perfectly monitoring Charlie for the last year. It's connected via wifi, so we can see (and hear) Charlie on our phones from anywhere in the house (or world for that matter). We can also make the camera move left, right, up, or down from our phones, and we can even talk to him through it. It's worked perfectly fine, and I have yet to find reason to purchase a $300 one. Point is, retailers prey on the fact that parents will pay a premium for the comfort of thinking their camera was made *specifically* for a baby, even if it's the same exact camera they market under another name to monitor death-row inmates. Keep that in mind is all I'm saying.

Walker: These are the little seats on wheels, usually with a little table attached, so the little one can scoot themselves around a room before they can walk. Some doctors don't recommend these anymore because of the fact that they allow babies to move faster and farther than they would naturally move on their own, which can lead to accidents (e.g. baby scoots along at full speed and bangs their head against the bottom of a dinner table). Walkers are also said to maybe delay the development of walking since they get the baby used to 'walking' without really having to balance themselves. All that said though, we used a walker with our baby, and loved it. It allowed him to have mobility (which he loved), and autonomy (which he also loved). As babies develop, they grow tired of the stages they reach and yearn for new ones. The walker was a great stage for Charlie; one that kept him engaged and occupied (and not crying) for quite a while. So in summary, I would recommend a walker, with the caveat that babies should be carefully supervised while in them.

Milk Warmer: You're going to be handling breast milk. Lots of it. Or perhaps formula. Either way, you're going to be in charge of the dosage and temperature of baby's only sustenance at all hours of the day and night. Because of this, I was very fond of a steam bottle warmer that we received as a gift. It looks kind of like a small coffee maker. You fill a little water reservoir that it uses to create steam, you insert the bottle of cold milk, twist the timing knob, and voila; in two minutes you've got perfectly warm milk ready to feed. No stovetops, no pans, nothing. I give this thing two thumbs way up.

Swaddling Blankets: We "borrowed" a few from the hospital (with a nurse's consent, of course); and we use them to this day.

Page 17, MASTITIS: Ok, so, the baby has been with you for a few weeks, you're almost used to the sleep deprivation; hey, you might even be starting to get the hang of this parenting stuff! And then boom: Mom gets a fever of 103 and can't get out of bed, leaving you to basically take care of the kid by yourself. This is when you realize just how truly and utterly unprepared you really are to handle things on your own. This happens. Mastitis is a bacterial infection that occurs when mom's milk ducts get infected. She has to stay in bed and take antibiotics (just what new moms want to ingest when they're breastfeeding!). There's many remedies and recommended ways to prevent mastitis, at the first sign (usually starts with tender, swollen breasts), you should talk to your doctor and figure out the best course of action.

Pages 18–28, THE (SOMETIMES) LACK OF IMMEDIATE CONNECTION ISSUE: Okay, so I didn't want to make a big fuss about this by including it in the title or on the cover or anything, but the subject matter covered in these pages is mostly what prompted me to write this book. It was a recurring sentiment repeated to me by some male friends with babies; a phenomenon I had never before read or heard about: the fact that many men don't feel an instant connection with their baby. I was told (privately) by several friends that *for months* they felt no meaningful connection with their baby; that they, conversely, felt close to nothing for their baby at first. Even worse, once the baby disrupted their daily lives so immensely without giving much back to them, some of my friends described feeling actual disillusionment, maybe even regret. And to make it worse, they felt so guilty, ashamed and embarrassed about these negative feelings that they hid them completely. After all, when has anyone seen a new dad on TV or a in a movie look at his newborn baby and not have his heart melt?

After hearing my friends describe these feelings, I started to do a little research online and found that this phenomenon is much more prevalent than one would expect. There were men all over the internet describing how they felt completely left out during the first few months while their spouses shared a clear physical and emotional connection with their babies.

The fact is, many men feel exactly that. And guess what? It's normal. As a man, you don't get to experience nearly the same physical connection with baby that mom does. You haven't carried the little guy/gal in your belly for nine months. You don't breastfeed several times a day. Biologically, the baby's need for you is different than for mom.

This is not to say that all men feel somewhat disconnected—not by a longshot. I have plenty of friends who were struck by a lightning bolt when they first laid eyes on their newborn and have remained in love ever since. That's totally normal too. The point of this passage is to let you know that we are all different, and that's okay. If you don't have that immediate connection, you shouldn't worry, or feel bad; you are not abnormal or weird.

And here's the good news: if you are one of those guys who doesn't feel that connection immediately, don't worry, you will. I promise you, eventually that little tadpole is going to take over your heart; he/she will be the thing you wake up for, the thing you daydream about, the thing you miss most when you're away. Trust me, it'll happen.

That's not to say it won't be tough; raising a baby is one hell of a job. There's going to be frustration, there's going to be fights, and there's going to be fear. This fear may come in many forms: fear of the commitment, fear of the responsibility, hell, even fear of just plain killing the thing (if you're anything like me, you'll probably spend many sleepless hours going back to the baby monitor over and over just to make sure he/she is still breathing). But believe me, all that stuff will pale in comparison to the joy.

I'd keep writing, but all this talk has me missing my boy. I'm gonna go play with the little guy now, see if I can finally get him to wave hello.

Fare thee well, gentlemen, and try to enjoy the ride.

C.P.

About the Author

Here I am with my wife Meredith, our son Charlie, and our dog Toby. Meredith is an actor (feel free to reach out if you have a "project" you think she'd be "right" for). Her only vice is coffee, which she can't rise without. I, on the other hand, have never had a cup of coffee. Or tea for that matter. Charlie's vice is putting in his mouth anything that if ingested might kill him. Toby can eat a tin can and be fine. He enjoys surfing, riding on my scooter, and chasing birds on the beach. Also, his full name is Toblerone VonDusseldorf.